Bear Grylls

SURVIVAL SKILLS HANDBOOK

DANGEROUS PLANTS

Bear Grylls

This survival handbook has been specially put together to help young adventurers just like you to stay safe in the wild. When you are out in the wild, you will come across many different plants – some are very helpful, but others can be incredibly dangerous. This book will show you how to identify some of the most dangerous plants, but beware never to eat anything in the wild unless you are 100 percent sure it is safe – it's better to be safe than sorry!

Bear

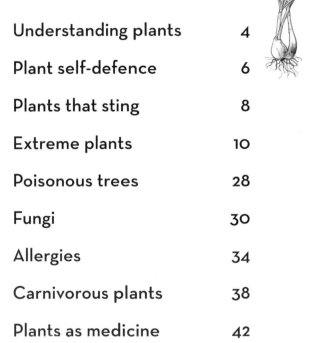

CONTENTS

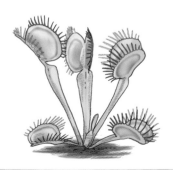

UNDERSTANDING PLANTS

While exploring you are likely to come across lots of different plants. Plants can be extremely useful for explorers but can also be deadly – it is important to learn as much as possible so that you can stay safe and take advantage of the useful kinds. Once you have some basic information you can use plants for tracking, as well as finding water, medicine, shelter, and food. They are also extremely interesting and enjoyable to study.

Plant safety

It takes many years of study to accurately identify plants – if you aren't one hundred percent sure what a plant is, don't touch it.

BEAR SAYS

If you are interested in foraging, the best way to learn is to go on an organised course with an expert.

Plant safety

- Always check with an adult who knows about plants before touching anything.
- If you are out exploring with your dog, keep it away from plants.
- Wash your hands after touching plants and before eating.
- Never eat any plant unless you have been told it is safe by an adult who is experienced in foraging and plant identification.
- Watch out for thorns, prickles, or the sharp edges of leaves. It is often tempting to run your hands up a tall reed or grass leaf only to get an injury similar to a paper cut.
- Be careful around water – sometimes pond weed can look like grass!
- Don't rub your eyes – some pollen can be extremely irritating.

be careful handing long grass

always check with an adult

always wash your hands after touching plants

PLANT SELF-DEFENCE

Plants can't run away, so they have developed ways to protect themselves from being eaten or destroyed by animals. Plants are clever multi-taskers too – for example, cacti may use their spines as shade or insulation, and to protect themselves from being eaten.

Thorns

Thorns are essentially stems that have been changed slightly to form a stiff and sharp growth. They contain tiny tubes that transport water and nutrients around the plant.

Spines

These are modified leaves and usually have transport tubes for water and nutrients. Some people prefer to group thorns and spines together as they are so similar.

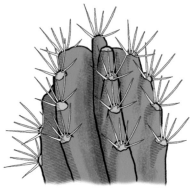

Prickles

Prickles are a bit like very coarse hairs. They do not have transport tubes and are easy to remove compared to a thorn or a spine. Roses have prickles, not thorns.

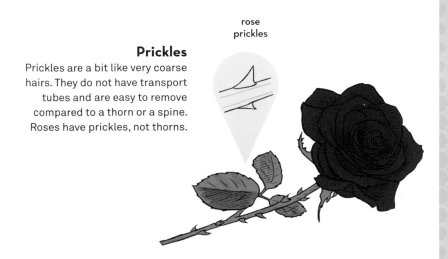

rose prickles

Neurotoxins

Star fruit contains a chemical that is a deadly neurotoxin for people with kidney disease. Healthy people can clear this chemical from their bodies without any problems, but for people with kidney disease this toxin builds up and eventually enters the brain. It can be deadly in extreme cases, so this usually yummy treat should be avoided.

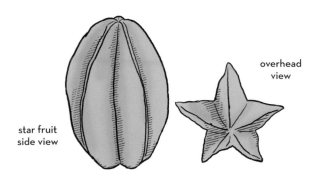

overhead view

star fruit side view

PLANTS THAT STING

Euphorbia
(danger rating = medium)
This plant contains a latex-type sap that can
irritate skin. Some people will experience no
reaction at all, but for others it can cause a rash,
blisters, pain, and even permanent scarring.
It can vary depending upon which variety of
euphorbia you touch – some types will be more
irritating than others. If this sap gets in the
eyes it can cause blindness in extreme cases.
People who have a latex allergy are more likely
to have a bad reaction to this plant. If you have
been irritated by this plant you need to ask a
grown up for medical advice. They may give you
antihistamines (a hayfever medicine) to stop the
itching. If it gets in your eyes, ask a grown up for
help with eye washing and check if you need to
see a doctor.

Geranium
(danger rating = low)
These plants are extremely common and
rarely cause much more than a minor
rash. They are found in most UK gardens
and are also often an indoor plant. Some
people may find that they need to wear
gloves when handling them.

Stinging nettle

(danger rating = low)

This plant is widespread in many countries, and can be found on most country walks and beside roads. Small children usually learn to identify this plant early on as it is often the same height as them and, if they fall into a patch, they can get badly stung. Tiny hairs break off into the skin and release a chemical that causes a bumpy rash and itching. If you get stung, it is worth looking for a patch of dock leaves – they often grow near to stinging nettles and contain chemicals that can cool down and neutralise a sting. Rub a dock leaf onto the rash.

nettle

dock leaf

BEAR SAYS

Always tell an adult if you are stung by a plant, especially if there is a rash or you feel unwell. If it doesn't get better, tell them again.

EXTREME PLANTS

Some plants are so sharp they can cause a serious injury if touched – and can even damage machinery.

BEAR SAYS

Avoid touching anything that someone tells you will hurt you – it's really tempting to touch and see how sharp it really is, but a painful injury can spoil a nice day out.

Prickly pear
(danger rating = low)
These are found in abundance in Mexico and in the Rocky Mountains in North America, but can also be seen in Australia, the Mediterranean, and South Africa. The fruit of the prickly pear, called "cactus fruit", is edible but must be peeled carefully! The spines can be removed by burning them off over a fire. Its pulp and juice are used to treat wounds and inflammation of the digestive and urinary system in Mexican folk medicine.

Jumping cactus
(danger rating = medium)
This is sometimes called the "teddy bear cholla", as it has small, fuzzy branches that look like teddy bear arms. However, it's not as cuddly as it looks. Pieces of the plant appear to jump from the plant onto anybody who brushes past it, and the spines are extremely painful. The segmented joint separates very easily from the main plant, and this is how the plant propagates – the broken off pieces will take root when they land, and use passing animals to transport the pieces away from the parent plant. You might find this cactus on desert treks.

Thorn tree of Africa (acacia)

(danger rating = low)

This tree has fierce thorns to deter predators. This defence works well, as the plant can grow to 6 m tall. However, it is still eaten by tall animals like giraffes, elephants, and gerenuks, whose special skeletons allow them to stand on their hind legs all day!

Goathead plant

(danger rating = low)

Also called the puncturevine weed, it has viciously pointed fruit called burrs that can puncture bicycle tyres and shoes with thin soles. The leaves and stems can be poisonous to livestock, and the burrs can cause physical damage. It grows in many dry climate locations around the world, often surviving in places where few other plants can grow.

Poison hemlock

(danger rating = high)

This is a highly poisonous flowering plant of the carrot family. It is sometimes called "devil's porridge", and is found in many parts of the word in poorly drained soil such as streams, ditches, and by the roadside. If an adult ate between six and eight leaves (or an even smaller amount of the seed or root) they could die. It paralyses the respiratory muscles, so one way to help someone who has been poisoned by this plant is to put them on a ventilator for two or three days until the effects wear off.

larks and quails eat this plant but they do not get poisoned, instead becoming poisonous themselves

☓ BEAR SAYS

Hemlock looks very similar to cow parsley, which is harmless. If in any doubt, do not touch! If you accidentally touch it, wash your hands immediately.

Water hemlock

(danger rating = high)

This is often confused with poison hemlock as it looks very similar and has a similar name. The only way to tell them apart is by looking at their roots. It's also poisonous and can cause seizures and sometimes death. It is considered one of North America's most poisonous plants. If you suspect someone has eaten either of these plants, it is vital to get them immediate medical attention.

Socrates

Socrates was a philosopher – he asked people to question their beliefs and knowledge. Lots of people didn't like him, and he was sent to prison and condemned to death. In ancient Greece, hemlock was often used to kill condemned prisoners. It was given to Socrates as a drink, and he died in 399 BCE.

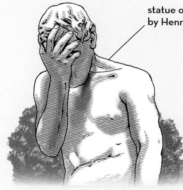

statue of Cain by Henri Vidal

Cain and Abel

In the Old Testament of the Bible, Cain, the son of Adam and Eve, murdered his brother Abel. There is a legend that hemlock has purple streaks on its stem to represent the Mark of Cain that God gave him as punishment.

Deadly nightshade

(danger rating = high)

This is part of the nightshade family, which also includes tomatoes and potatoes. It is found from the UK in the West, to parts of Iran in the East, as well as some parts of the U.S. and Canada. The leaves and berries are extremely toxic and can cause very unpleasant hallucinations. Their attractive appearance is misleading – they are in fact highly poisonous. This has led to some people becoming poisoned after eating them. The root is usually the most toxic part of the plant. Strangely, cattle and rabbits don't appear to be affected when they eat it.

Deadly nightshade is commonly known as belladonna, meaning "beautiful lady". People used to drop it in their eyes to make their pupils dilate (get bigger), as this was considered attractive. Unfortunately, this caused unpleasant side effects, including blindness, so the plant is no longer used in this way.

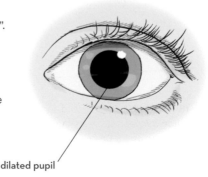

dilated pupil

In 2012, a German monk was found wandering naked in a forest. He had eaten some deadly nightshade berries while camping, and had become confused. He was taken to hospital to be treated.

A mother began hallucinating after eating a ham sandwich. She later realised that her daughter was being treated with atropine (a type of eye medication extracted from deadly nightshade) and the bottle of eye drops had fallen over in the fridge, dripping onto the meat.

In 1846, a herb gatherer sold some deadly nightshade berries that were made into pies. Tragically, a man and a three-year-old boy died after eating them.

White snakeroot

(danger rating = high)

This plant, found in parts of America, contains a toxin called tremetol that can get into cows' meat and milk if they eat it. If this contaminated milk is drunk by a human, they can develop a condition called "milk sickness". Due to changes in production methods and the way cows are bred, milk sickness has become extremely uncommon.

this cow is eating white snakeroot, and will become contaminated

Nancy Hanks Lincoln

Nancy was the mother of Abraham Lincoln, the president of the U.S. from 1861 to 1865. She died in 1818, when Abraham was nine, from what is thought to have been milk sickness. Thousands in the Midwest died from this illness before the cause was understood.

BEAR SAYS

Other names for this deadly plant include richweed, tall boneset, and white sanicle.

Medical uses

White snakeroot may be poisonous, but it also has many helpful uses. A tea made from the plant has been used in the past as a cure for diarrhea, sickness, fever, and kidney stones. It has also been reported to cure bites from some snakes.

Though many plants have medical uses, never try this yourself. If you are unwell, tell an adult and let them decide what to do.

Castor bean

(danger rating = high)

The castor bean is the seed of the castor oil plant, which is found in tropical regions such as the Mediterranean, East Africa, and India, and is grown as an ornamental plant in many other places. Castor oil can be extracted from the seed and has lots of uses including soap, dyes, paint, and as a laxative medicine. It also contains ricin, which is toxic. After the beans have been crushed to get the oil out, the ricin is left in the residue. Ricin is believed to be one of the most toxic naturally occurring substances. However, as it is difficult for the substance to get into the human body accidentally, it is unusual to find cases of ricin poisoning.

castor oil plant

inside the castor bean

false castor oil plant

BEAR SAYS

The false castor oil plant, *fatsia japonica*, looks very similar to the castor oil plant, but it isn't related.

Poison from the castor bean plant usually gets into the body by one of three methods: ingestion, inhalation, or injection.

1. Ingestion. Ricin is extremely emetic (it makes you vomit) so most people will be sick and the ricin will just come out of the body again (although some people have still died by swallowing it).

2. Inhaling (breathing in) even a tiny amount of ricin can be fatal, but as ricin particles are quite large they can only travel a short distance in the air before falling to the ground. This means it is unlikely that someone will accidentally inhale the substance.

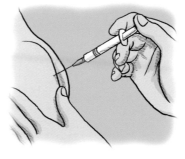

3. Injection (directly into the bloodstream). This is very unlikely to happen accidentally.

Georgi Markov

In 1978, Bulgarian journalist Georgi Markov was on his way to work at the BBC in London, UK. While he was waiting for a bus near Waterloo Bridge, he felt a sharp sting in the back of his leg. He looked round and saw a man pick up an umbrella and get into a taxi. He felt unwell that evening and died a few days later.

Georgi Markov

the umbrella was used to administer poisonous ricin

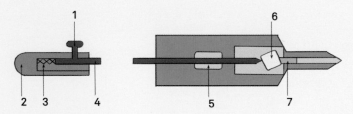

1. Trigger in umbrella handle
2. Umbrella handle
3. Spring to push linkage system
4. Linkage system linking trigger to valve
5. Cylinder of compressed air.
6. Switch that activates valve
7. Valve that fires ricin pellet through the "barrel" of the umbrella.

A spherical pellet the size of a pin head was found in Markov's leg. It had holes in it and contained ricin. The holes were blocked up with a substance designed to melt at body temperature, so that when the pellet entered Markov's body it released its deadly contents into his bloodstream. Markov was a writer, and the Bulgarian government are thought to have asked the Russian security service to help assassinate him because of his criticism of the communist regime. Nobody has been charged with his murder – it is thought that most documents relating to his death were destroyed.

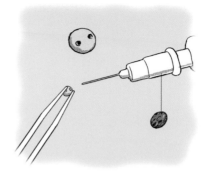

BEAR SAYS

This event is known as the "umbrella murder" and was very infamous at the time.

Vladimir Kostov

Another Bulgarian, Vladimir Kostov, was attacked in Paris 10 days before Markov by a man carrying a small bag. An identical pellet was found in his body, but he didn't die. It is thought that the special coating was damaged during the shot or before it was fired, and most of the ricin had leaked away before entering his body.

Rosary pea

(danger rating = high)

Rosary peas contain a deadly poison that is a close relative of ricin. The plant grows in tropical and sub-tropical areas of the world, but is originally from India. These attractive peas have traditionally been used in jewellery around the world, especially rosaries. A rosary is a string of beads that are used by Catholics to keep count when saying a set of prayers. There are reports that the workers who make holes in the beads to string them together have been poisoned. If you ever buy jewellery made from seeds it's worth checking they aren't rosary peas.

necklace made from
rosary peas

Oleander

(danger rating = high)

Oleander is widely cultivated, and nobody is sure exactly where it is originally from. It is one of the most poisonous commonly grown garden plants, and all parts of it are toxic. The foliage may cause irritation if it touches your skin and if it is eaten it can cause all sorts of nasty effects, including death. Luckily, the flowers have no nectar, so it is unlikely that the poison would contaminate the honey as bees are uninterested in the plant. It is often found in parks. Oleander has been documented in the past as being used as a medicine for all sorts of illnesses, and it is currently being researched to see if extracts of the plant could be useful in medicine today.

BEAR SAYS

Oleander is the official flower of the city of Hiroshima, Japan, as it was the first plant to bloom after atomic bombs were dropped in 1945.

Roman soldiers

Oleander was used by Roman soldiers as a hangover cure.

Pliny

Pliny was a Roman natural historian who wrote an encylopedia that became a model for the ones we use today. Pliny wrote that oleander was useful as "an antidote against the venom of serpents".

Tobacco

(danger rating = high)

Tobacco is widely grown around the world, but China is currently the top producer. Dried tobacco leaves are mainly used for smoking. People who smoke are far more likely to suffer diseases such as cancer than people who don't smoke. Tobacco contains nicotine, a stimulant that makes tobacco highly addictive.

tobacco leaf

tobacco plant

BEAR SAYS

Nicotine is very addictive, and the long-term effects of smoking can be deadly, so it's best never to start.

Nicotine poisoning

If you swallow, inhale, or touch nicotine, it is possible to get nicotine poisoning. Although it is potentially deadly, serious overdoses are rare. People who die from nicotine poisoning usually do so within four hours of exposure.

Effects of smoking on the body

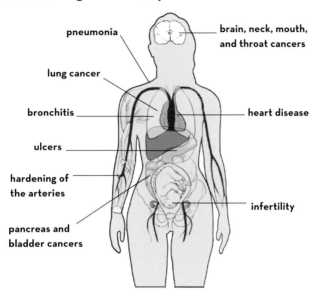

pneumonia

brain, neck, mouth, and throat cancers

lung cancer

bronchitis

heart disease

ulcers

hardening of the arteries

infertility

pancreas and bladder cancers

Green tobacco sickness

This is a type of nicotine poisoning that is caused by skin contact with wet tobacco leaves. It is mainly experienced by people who harvest tobacco crops. Workers who already smoke are less likely to get this sickness, but are much more likely to get all sorts of other diseases.

the tobacco in an e-cigarette can be hazardous to children if they accidentally swallow or touch it

Wolf's bane (aconitum)

(danger rating = high)

Also known as monkshood or devil's helmet, this plant is found in the Northern Hemisphere in mountainous areas. It is a deadly poison. It has been used to make poison arrows for hunting. If poisoning is fatal, the victim will usually die within two to six hours. It can cause poisoning if handled without gloves, as it is easily absorbed by the skin. Symptoms may include tingling and numbness, and the heart can be affected. Immediate first aid is needed for anyone who has accidentally eaten or touched this plant.

wolf's bane flowers

wolf's bane roots

wolf's bane plant

BEAR SAYS

In 2009, a woman was sent to prison for poisoning a man after she put aconite (another name for wolf's bane) in his dinner.

Poison ivy

(danger rating = medium)

This grows throughout much of North America and some parts of Asia. The sap from this plant will cause a rash on anyone who touches it. Poison ivy is not a true ivy, but is actually a member of the cashew family. The leaves turn from green to red in the autumn, so its appearance varies depending on the season.

poison ivy
plant

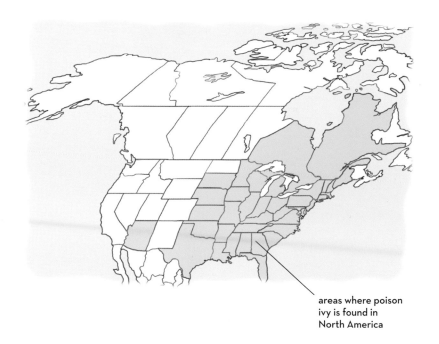

areas where poison
ivy is found in
North America

POISONOUS TREES

There are many trees that can be dangerous to humans and livestock, with leaves, flowers, fruit, and sap that can be poisonous. Be very careful when collecting wood or foliage, as some trees can cause serious harm.

laburnham leaves

Laburnham trees
(danger rating = medium)
These trees contain a poison that is similar to nicotine. All parts of the tree are poisonous, but the biggest hazards are the seed pods, which are often mistaken for pea pods. The poison is rarely fatal, but can cause bad stomach pains and vomiting if eaten.

laburnham seed pods

laburnham flowers

BEAR SAYS

Laburnham trees are a food source for buff tip moths, that camouflage themselves to look like a silver birch twig.

buff tip moth

Cebera odollam

(danger rating = high)

This highly toxic plant grows across India and South East Asia, and has caused many deaths – possibly even murders. It contains a strong toxin that affects the heart, but it is very difficult to detect traces in the body. The toxin is contained within a kernel inside the fruit. It tastes bitter, but the taste can be disguised by spicy food.

cebera odollam fruit

Yew tree

(danger rating = high)

Wood from the yew tree was once used to make bows for firing arrows. This tree has many poisonous parts, including the seeds, which are highly toxic. If ingested, victims can die within hours without displaying any symptoms. This can make the poison difficult to detect without testing.

yew tree berries

FUNGI

Fungi isn't a plant or an animal, but a separate group altogether, that includes yeast, moulds, and mushrooms. It is estimated that there are between 1.5 and 5 million species of fungi, and there is lots still to learn about them. They can be edible and useful in medicine but can also be extremely dangerous – never pick or eat them in the wild.

BEAR SAYS

It is never worth taking the risk of foraging for mushrooms unless you are an experienced expert – they can kill. Stay away!

Death cap
(danger rating = high)
This is one of the world's deadliest mushrooms. It looks very similar to many edible mushrooms and tastes quite pleasant, but one mushroom is enough to kill. It is mainly seen in autumn, and people who eat it can suffer from serious liver damage that may cause death.

Destroying angel

(danger rating = high)

These white mushrooms are sometimes confused with puff-balls and other edible mushrooms. Half a mushroom can kill and the toxin can cause liver and kidney failure. Cooking it does not destroy the poison. The diagram below shows the different areas of the body affected by the toxin.

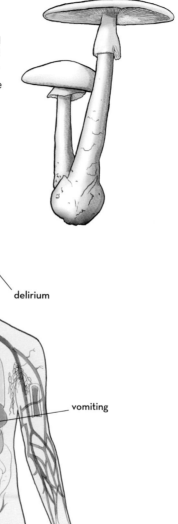

delirium

liver damage

kidney damage

vomiting

Fly agaric

(danger rating = high)

This mushroom is red with white spots – just like in cartoons. It may look pretty, but it is toxic. If eaten it can cause hallucinations (when someone thinks they can see something that isn't really there).

fly agaric mushrooms

hallucinations can be very dangerous

Jack o'lantern

(danger rating = high)

This poisonous fungus looks similar to chanterelle mushrooms, which are edible. It can be found on dead trees in Europe. It is not usually lethal, but can make you feel very unwell if it is eaten.

jack o'lantern mushrooms

BEAR SAYS

If you think you have eaten a poisonous mushroom, tell an adult and seek medical help immediately.

chanterelle mushroom

ALLERGIES

When the human body has a reaction to a particular food or substance it is called an allergy. Allergies can go away as a child gets older or can develop later in adulthood. One quarter of people suffer from an allergy at some point in their lives. Luckily, severe allergies are rare and most can be kept under control with careful management.

pollen particles

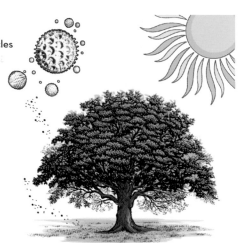

Hayfever

This common allergy is caused by grass and tree pollen. Hayfever can cause sneezing, a runny nose, and itchy eyes. It is less of a problem in winter as heavier rainfall helps keep lower levels of pollen in the air. There is no cure, but treatment is available to control it.

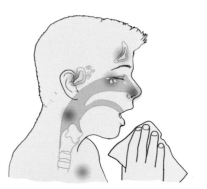

hayfever symptoms include coughing, sneezing, and red, itchy eyes

BEAR SAYS

If you think you have an allergy to something, it is important to discuss it with your doctor to get the correct advice.

34

Avoiding hayfever
If you are sensitive to hayfever, these tips can help minimise side effects:

- If you have medication, make sure you take it and follow the instructions carefully – don't forget to pack it if you are going away.
- Check the pollen count before you go on a hike or walk.
- Stay away from grassy areas and people mowing the grass, and consider postponing camping trips at times when the pollen count is high if your hayfever is severe.
- Wear wraparound sunglasses to keep pollen out of your eyes.
- Shower and change your clothes after being outdoors if possible.
- Keep vehicle windows closed.
- Dust and hoover regularly – dusting with a damp duster catches more pollen than using a dry one.
- Tell an adult if you feel unwell.

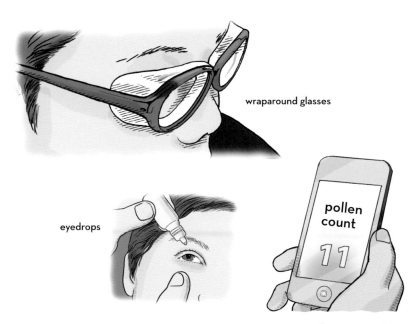

wraparound glasses

eyedrops

pollen count

11

pollen count can be checked online

Food allergies

Nuts, fruit, shellfish, eggs, and cows' milk are commonly associated with food allergies. Allergic reactions can be life-threatening, but are often mild. Food allergies can cause an itchy mouth, throat, or ears, swelling, a rash, or vomiting. Anaphylaxis is life-threatening and the symptoms include difficulty breathing, light headedness, and loss of consciousness. Some people with food allergies have an auto-injector pen, commonly known as an EpiPen®, that contains a hormone called adrenaline that can be used in emergencies.

BEAR SAYS

It's well worth taking a first aid course as CPR needs to be taught. If you are on an organised trip with adults, someone should be qualified in first aid.

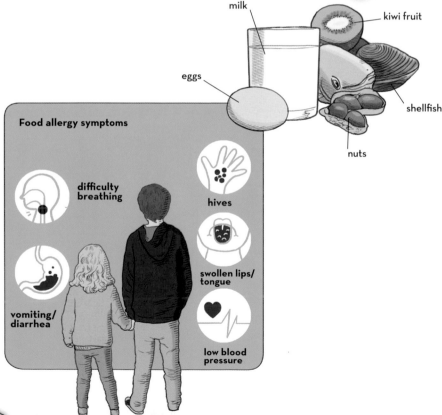

Common causes of allergies

milk

kiwi fruit

eggs

shellfish

nuts

Food allergy symptoms

difficulty breathing

hives

swollen lips/ tongue

vomiting/ diarrhea

low blood pressure

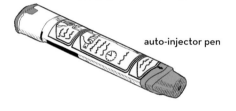

First aid for food allergies

A person with a food allergy should try and prevent any problems by avoiding foods they know causes them harm. Here are a few top tips to help someone suffering from an allergic reaction:

- Call for an adult and/or medical help even if the symptoms are mild or have stopped.
- Call emergency services to explain that you think someone is having a severe allergic reaction, and tell the operator what you think has caused it.
- If the person has medication such as an auto-injector pen (EpiPen®) help them use it.
- Place them into a comfortable sitting position, leaning slightly forward to help their breathing.
- If they become unresponsive, clear their airway and check their breathing.
- If they aren't breathing, CPR (chest compressions and rescue breaths) will need to be performed until medical help arrives.

mobile phone and powerbank

auto-injector pen

Allergies in the wild

If you are planning a trip outdoors, follow these tips to stay safe:

- Take a charged mobile phone and a powerbank if possible.
- Always tell someone your route and when you expect to get home – that way, if something goes wrong they can get help. Don't go out on your own.
- Don't eat or touch anything you aren't sure about.
- Wash your hands regularly.
- Make sure you have taken any medication you need, and have enough with you for your trip.
- If someone starts to get unwell, get help immediately.
- Make sure other people know about any allergies and what to do in an emergency.

CARNIVOROUS PLANTS

Carnivorous plants trap animals (usually insects) and consume them to get nutrients.

Five main trapping methods

1. Carnivorous plants often have an adhesive (sticky) surface that keeps hold of insects that touch the plant's surface.

2. More sophisticated carnivorous plants have slightly more elegant traps, such as the pitfall trap (see right). Here, the leaves are shaped like cups or pots and may have a slippery surface along the edges, an adhesive layer, and possibly even a liquid to drown insects trapped inside.

3. The lobster pot is another sophisticated trap. Plants like the corkscrew plant have an entrance that is easy to locate by the insect on the outside, but once inside it is difficult to find its way out again. This technique is so effective at fooling prey that humans have adopted a similar trap for catching lobsters, hence the name lobster trap.

4. Some carnivorous plants have extremely sensitive hairs on their leaves. They use these to catch their prey by snapping shut once they sense an insect touching a leaf. This trap has been appropriately named the "snap trap".

5. The final and most sophisticated trap in the plant kingdom is the bladder trap. Plants that use the bladder trap suck in their prey by pumping out water to increase pressure inside the plant. Once the plant senses an insect, it springs out and sucks in the insect with the built-up pressure inside the plant pulling in the insect.

snap trap

Attenborough's pitcher plant

This species of pitfall plant is named after British naturalist and broadcaster Sir David Attenborough. It is found in the Philippines.

pitcher plant

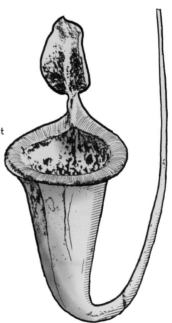

BEAR SAYS

Pitcher plants are sometimes known as "monkey cups" as monkeys have been seen drinking from them.

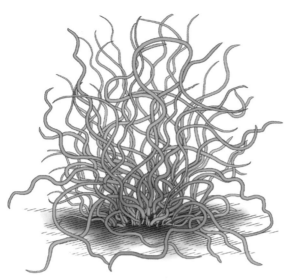

Corkscrew plant

These lobster pot plants grow in Africa and Central and South America. The corkscrew trap is underground and is actually a leaf not a root. They trap tiny, single-celled animals called protozoa.

Venus flytrap

This is probably the best known carnivorous plant. It traps insects and spiders, but doesn't digest them until it "feels" them wriggle around. It's so sensitive that it can tell the difference between raindrops and prey. The hair-like structures on the edge of the trap prevent larger prey escaping, but allow smaller prey to escape as they aren't worth digesting.

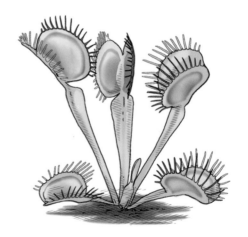

Bladder trap plants

Bladderworts are common across every continent except Antarctica. They commonly trap small organisms under the ground or water surface by sucking them in when they brush against trigger hairs. They are found in very wet soil or in ponds and streams.

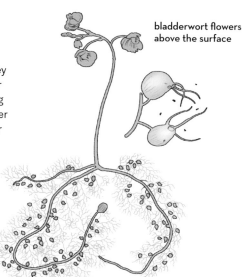

bladderwort flowers above the surface

bladder traps below the surface

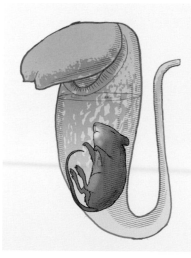

The good news is that, despite looking quite scary, carnivorous plants are not dangerous to humans. The largest animal known to be consumed by some of the larger pitfall traps is a rat, and even that is rare.

PLANTS AS MEDICINE

Plants have been used as medicine for many thousands of years. Developments in modern science allow us to better understand the positive and negative effects plants have on the human body. Some old remedies are still used today as they are still effective, but others are no longer used, having been replaced by modern medicines.

Ancient Egyptians

We know a lot about the history of medicine in Egypt from the translation of some ancient medical documents including the Ebers Papyrus. Ancient Egyptians chewed willow bark to relieve fever and headaches. Aspirin is a modern medicine for fever and headaches and contains a chemical found in willow bark.

ancient Egyptian medical texts

foxglove plant

Foxgloves

(danger rating = high)

Foxgloves are poisonous in small amounts – they cause the heart to slow down, and the victim to vomit. However, modern medicine has developed ways of using extracts from this plant to safely treat certain heart conditions, such as congestive heart failure.

BEAR SAYS

Never chew willow bark if you have a headache – tell an adult instead and let them decide what to do.

Madagascar periwinkle

(danger rating = low)

In 1960 the survival rate of childhood leukaemia (a type of cancer) was around 10 percent. It is now over 90 percent. This is largely because of the Madagascar periwinkle. A chemical compound was discovered in the plant that is used to treat cancer and is considered one of the most important medical breakthroughs of the 20th century.

Madagascar periwinkle

Alexander Fleming

Antibiotics from fungi

Although fungi don't belong to the plant kingdom, they are important to know about and so are included here. In 1929, a Scottish scientist called Alexander Fleming was trying to find a treatment for infected wounds when he made one of the biggest discoveries in modern medicine. On one of the agar plates (special glass dishes) used in his experiments, Alexander noticed that that the bacteria on the dish couldn't grow around a spot of the fungus. This was an incredible discovery as bacteria is the main cause of infection for wounds. Two other British scientists worked together to explore this discovery by identifying the useful component in fungi, and used it to save many lives in the Second World War – and ever since. The medicine they discovered is known as penicillin. All three scientists received the Nobel Prize for their work in 1945.

Quinine

(danger rating = low)

Malaria is caused by a bite from a mosquito infected by the malaria disease. There are hundreds of millions of people infected with malaria every year, and it is common in hot climate regions around the Equator. It causes a nasty illness that can be treated with quinine from the bark of the cinchona tree (also known as the fever tree). The science behind how it works isn't yet completely understood.

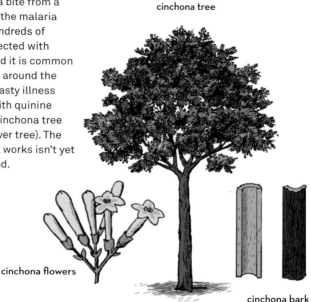

cinchona tree

cinchona flowers

cinchona bark

Daffodils

(danger rating = medium)

Alzheimer's disease, which causes dementia, might be treated in the future with a drug made from daffodil bulbs. Scientists are currently developing this new medicine.

daffodil bulbs

GLOSSARY

Botanical name – the formal scientific name of a plant.

Carnivorous – meat-eating.

Continent – a large landmass on Earth.

Encyclopaedia – a reference book or website that contains lots of information about some or all areas of knowledge.

Equator – an imaginary line dividing the Earth into two halves, exactly halfway between the North and South Poles.

Hallucinating – experiencing sensations that appear real but are created by your mind.

Identifying – recognising what something is.

Inflammation – the body's response to something harmful, usually felt as heat, pain, redness, or swelling.

Insulation – a material that stops heat from spreading.

Kernels – the central soft part of a nut, seed, or fruit stone.

Latex – a milky fluid found in many plants.

Neurotoxin – a poison that acts on the brain, spinal cord, and the nerves.

Northern Hemisphere – the half of the Earth that is north of the Equator.

Nutrient – a component of food that is used to survive and grow.

Stimulant – something that makes you more active or gives you more energy.

Sub-tropical area – an area that borders a hot and humid tropical area.

Toxin – a poison capable of causing injury or death.

Urinary system – kidneys, bladder, and tubes that work together to remove waste from the blood and produce urine.

Vomiting – being sick.

Discover more amazing books in the Bear Grylls series:

Perfect for young adventurers, the
Survival Skills Handbook series
accompanies an exciting range of
colouring and activity books. Curious
kids can also learn tips and tricks
for almost any extreme situation in
Survival Camp, and explore Earth in
Extreme Planet.

Conceived by Weldon Owen in partnership
with Bear Grylls Ventures

Produced by Weldon Owen Ltd
Suite 3.08 The Plaza, 535 King's Road,
London SW10 0SZ, UK

WELDON OWEN LTD
Publisher Donna Gregory
Designer Shahid Mahmood
Editors Claire Philip, Susie Rae, Lydia Halliday
Editorial assistant Thomas McBrien
Contributor Anne Farthing
Illustrator Bernard Chau

Disclaimer
Weldon Owen and Bear Grylls take pride in doing our best to get the facts right in putting together
the information in this book, but occasionally something slips past our beady eyes. Therefore we
make no warranties about the accuracy or completeness of the information in the book and to the
maximum extent permitted, we disclaim all liability. Wherever possible, we will endeavour to correct
any errors of fact at reprint.

Kids – if you want to try any of the activities in this book, please ask your parents first! Parents – all
outdoor activities carry some degree of risk and we recommend that anyone participating in these
activities be aware of the risks involved and seek professional instruction and guidance. None of the
health/medical information in this book is intended as a substitute for professional medical advice;
always seek the advice of a qualified practitioner.

A WELDON OWEN PRODUCTION. AN IMPRINT OF KINGS ROAD PUBLISHING
PART OF THE BONNIER PUBLISHING GROUP.